Image courtesy of James Randolph

Michael Quigley, BA (Hons) 1st class, MA, PGCE, is a former primary school teacher with extensive experience of teaching, coaching, leading and team membership, coupled with a life-long enduring passion for and interest in fitness, wellbeing, personal formation and fulfilment. This book lays out the Kataholos Philosophy, which aims to enable people to live a wholistic full life in mind, body, spirit, emotional and digital health.

This book is for my world family. The entire people of the world, to whom my life is one of service, gratitude and love. To my wonderful family, especially my mum, who has always been my number one supporter.
And to my dear departed friend, Father Peter Robertson – you showed me what a good man was.

Michael Quigley

KATAHOLOS: GUIDELINES FOR A WHOLISTIC HAPPY LIFE

AUSTIN MACAULEY PUBLISHERS™

LONDON • CAMBRIDGE • NEW YORK • SHARJAH

A CIP catalogue record for this title is available from the British Library.

ISBN 9781528905305 (Paperback)
ISBN 9781528905312 (E-Book)

www.austinmacauley.com

First Published (2018)
Austin Macauley Publishers Ltd
25 Canada Square
Canary Wharf
London
E14 5LQ

I would like to acknowledge the men and women who have helped to bring me to this wonderful place – Mrs Wood and Kevin Treston – wonderful teachers. My parents, Kevin and Kathleen, who always act with integrity. A huge thank you to my very talented brother, Peter, for his fantastic art work both on the cover and throughout the book.

And to the thousands of books I have read; you have been my loves, my adventures, my teachers, my friends. It is my pleasure to add to your ranks.

Table of Content

Bonus Materials 83

Part 1
The Body

Here, you will find tips and suggestions to help you in the areas of the body, including fitness and nutrition. These are the principles I have found that work for me in my own life, take whatever you want and make it work for you.

Tip 1 – Weight Training Is a Must!

Whether it is using your own body weight, dumbbells, resistance bands or any of the other excellent options, this is my number 1 tip to help your body. I always had broad shoulders but was skinny fat and unsure of my body. Through weight training, I have been able to balance out my body so that it is more in proportion. For example, by building my shoulder and back muscles, my previously large chest is now in proportion to my other muscles and I no longer look like a stick that has swallowed a fridge and got it stuck in his lungs!

Weight training helps your body to burn more calories after exercise, which is a bonus. Also, I find great satisfaction in learning new exercises, improving my form and being able to lift more weight and for longer. You really do feel a sense of achievement. Bodybuilding to me just means sculpting your body so that it looks the way you want it and weights have helped me to achieve this. I've gotten stronger, leaned up and now I'm exploring using body weight exercises to do more advanced techniques like handstands, splits, callisthenics and breakdancing. Seriously, pick up some weights, lift carefully with good form and I guarantee the results will amaze you!

Make sure you work out your chest, back and legs first. These are the major muscle groups and working them brings great results! Your shoulders, arms, core and lower back are also important, and can be fitted in among your major muscle groups. Start with weight training two-three times a week for 20 minutes and build up slowly. Don't train for longer than 45 minutes with weights in your first year as the quality of your practise will go down the longer you do it past this point. Form is very important. Make sure you receive instruction on how to lift the weights; this is very important in the beginning when you will be unsure about what you are doing.

Tip 2 – Do Cardio

I'm a funny one for cardio. I know many runners, in fact my dad was a marathon runner. I also did Jiu-Jitsu for 12 years, which was great as a form of cardio. I swim, go running, climb and play football; I'll pretty much try anything. For me, cardio has three levels, the first of which you can always access, no matter what your fitness level is.

Level 1 – general movement, stretching and walking
A brisk walk for 20–30 minutes is a great fat burner. I never believed this until I tried it but it is true. The combination of fresh air, movement and nature can do wonders for your health. If this is the only form of cardio that you can do, it is still a great place to start.

Level 2 – running, swimming, dancing, climbing
These are the activities where you get nice, hot and sweaty. Just pick one that you enjoy and go for it! You can build up and go up quite quickly from one dance class a week to three in a few months, or doing 5 laps to 50 in the pool in the same amount of time.

Level 3 – martial arts, squash, hiking, rugby, sprint training
These are great for giving your body a blast of high intensity exercise. You will sweat a lot and your heart will really be hammering but that is a good thing. Just be careful and remember not to do these activities for as long as you would do the easier ones, i.e. for hours and hours. You will know when you are ready to do your cardio at this level and

you will get lots of fat burning and cardiovascular benefits from them.

Here's a suggested programme for beginners wanting to run:

Monday – 15 minute walk – alternating jogging with walking when you get out of breath
Tuesday – rest
Wednesday – 15 minute walk – alternative walking with jogging
Thursday – rest
Friday – big run for 20 minutes. Try to walk as little as possible
Saturday and Sunday – rest

I learned this for my dad. I learnt this from my dad. The idea is that you do three runs a week, which gives you four rest days, which is nicely balanced. Then you go for a longer run every three runs and stay at that level next week. For example, next week would be 20 minutes, 20 minutes and 25 minutes. The following week would be 25 minutes, 25 minutes and 30 minutes etc. By following this programme, you can be running for one hour in 9 weeks! So, to sum up, find something that you are interested in; there will be a class for it, or check it out online. Then start small and build up and your cardio ability will go up very quickly. Remember, if you are red, huffing and puffing and out of breath, it doesn't mean that you are unfit: you are working at exactly the level you need to.

Tip 3 – Measure Your Heart Rate

Your heart keeps you alive – simple as that. The slower the amount of times your heart beats in a minute, the fitter you are. A person in decent shape will have a heart rate in their 60s when they are resting and not doing any activity. While you are exercising and afterwards, expect it to rise quickly and dramatically. Athletes have a resting heart rate in their 40s, around 44 beats per minute.

One of the best ways of measuring your fitness is to measure your resting heart rate. It may be quite high at first, but the fitter you get, the stronger your heart becomes and so the less time it needs to beat per minute to pump blood around your body. It becomes a lot more efficient and the best way to do this is through exercise. My heart rate has come down recently from the mid-70s into the 60s and 50s and once, recently it even measured as 44. Athlete level! I was well chuffed!

So, get yourself a heart rate monitor for free online or as a downloadable app. Then just measure it each day, preferably around the same time and after exercise, just to see the difference. What you pay attention to grows and once you start to measure your rate, you will see big improvements in your health. Remember, your heart keeps you alive and if you look after it, it will keep you around for a long time to come.

Tip 4 – Nutrition

Put loads of good stuff into your body and a few bits of rubbish. Nice and simple. That's a way that most nutritionists, dieticians and doctors agree on. I have tried a variety of things: from cutting down on treats to bodybuilding nutrition, carb cycling, calorie counting and many others. There is no one specific optimal way to eat, but there are many excellent things that you can do to make sure your nutrition is brilliant.

Here are ten bulletproof nutritional nuggets:

1. Drink lots of water – four litres a day, if possible. Your body is made up of primarily water and most processes in your body take place in water, so you need loads of it. Don't worry about going to the toilet all the time, you'll get used to it. Your skin, nails, energy levels and bowel movements will improve and thank you for it.
2. Eat lots of different fruits and vegetables every day. I'm not going to put a number on the amount you should eat, the more the better. Try and eat more vegetables than fruit and eat a wide variety. Your

body needs that full variety, so go for all colours: red, yellow, white, green, orange, and purple. Each brings different combinations of vitamins and minerals which help your body in different ways. You can consume a massive amount of them, as they have a high-water content and are nutritionally dense but low in calories. A real winner!

3. Treat yourself to something tasty at least a few times a week. You need to feel that the way you are eating is enjoyable and sustainable, or you will be unhappy. If you have three meals a day, that's 21 in a week. So, if two of those are pizza or cake, that's okay, if the other 19 are healthy and nutritious. Where people fall is that they have one or two big cheat meals, feel really bad about it and think, *Oh, what's the point?* and give up. No, that is when you must endure. Otherwise, you will be continually restarting and you will never build any momentum or see any progress.

4. Make sure that you consume enough protein. Good protein sources include chicken, fish, beef, tofu, rice and peas, lamb and other meats. Nuts are also good for protein and are very high in good fats, but remember that they are very high in calories. If you go for a run, or visit the gym, make sure that you consume some protein afterwards to help your body recover from your workout. Make sure that you eat a portion of protein in each meal of breakfast, lunch and dinner. Also, if you are vegetarian, make sure that you eat enough beans, lentils, good soy and tofu. Protein is needed for every process in your body; from growing your hair to your nails, healthy eyes and skin as well as building muscles and helping the body to recover and rebuild after a workout.

5. Sweet stuff! I know it is really tasty but unless you are using it to help fuel you during an endurance event, your body really doesn't need it. Sure, it can taste good, but you need to start thinking beyond just how good it tastes. Unless you have just done a

workout, you don't need any sugar at all. However, once you have done a workout, drinking some protein with a spoon of sugar with it will allow the protein to attach itself to the sugar; to be absorbed more quickly into the body, like somebody hitching a lift to get there faster. But that does not mean you can lie around eating chocolates before bed just because you went out for a run earlier in the day.

6. Eat your carbohydrates doesn't need a large space here carbs – doesn't need a large space here carefully. Generally, we don't need to eat as much pasta, rice and bread as we think we do. If wholegrain, these can be good sources of fibre and protein, and if white versions, they will give you a shorter energy boost with less nutritional value. If you have done a big training session, then eat some pasta or rice to refuel afterwards, but if you haven't, then your body doesn't need it. It's quite a simple tip to remember. If you're wanting to cut down on how much you are eating in a day, start with decreasing your carbs slightly, and making sure to refuel only when you need to.

7. Learn to cook! The more you can cook, the more options and choice you have when you eat. So, if you enjoy porridge, learn to make it and you can have it every day! Just check out some free YouTube videos to get you started. I would personally recommend cooking books by the *Hairy Dieters* range, *Clean Eating Alice Eat Well Every Day,* books by The Body Coach, books by Sabrina Ghayour, *Vegan 100* by Gaz Oakley and any of the *River Cottage* books by Hugh Fernley-Whittingstall, to start off. There are many really tasty, healthy versions of your favourite treats available in books like *Chocolate Covered Katie,* where she substitutes using white sugar for xylitol, a diabetic friendly alternative. So, learn to cook, and you won't be relying on other people or situations to provide your food; you will very quickly have the

skills to cook and make for yourself healthy, tasty, nutritious food.

8. How much to eat? So, how much should you eat in a day? Well, the average calorie count for a man is currently recommended to be 2500 calories a day, and women 2000 calories a day. To lose weight, you will need to consume under this number every day and to gain weight; you will need to eat more. And the important thing is to do this consistently. If you eat 2500 calories as a man four days a week, but then 3000 for three, then the extra calories in those three days will mean you will gain weight, even though you ate the recommended amount for most amount of time. But that's a bit disheartening, so let's liven this up a bit! I've successfully built muscle and lost fat in my body, so I'll keep things simple and give you a formula that will get results in a month onwards. Firstly, don't worry about what the numbers on the scale say, focus on eating good food, looking good and feeling good. These are much better motivation and are sustainable.

Here is the formula for a woman to sensibly lose weight:

2000 calories a day – 20% of your calories is 400 less, so you would consume 1600 calories a day. Eating any less is too drastic and will not help you.

For a man to sensibly lose weight:

2500 calories a day – 20% of your calories is 500 less, so you would consume 2000 a day.

Make sure that once a while you eat more than this; to refuel your body and give yourself a break from the discipline of this. Like having an occasional treat, this will ensure that what you are doing is consistent and sustainable, which is very important. This will give you results, as early as one month in, when you stick to it.

9. Variety – eat a wide variety of different foods all the time. As we have covered, the good things to eat such as good protein, lots of fruit and vegetable, good carbs, water and occasional treats, let's look at why variety is so important. Your food needs to be like your life: exciting, interesting, fun, sometimes plain and sometimes crazy because that is what your body needs. It's basically a walking hangover from the age of the hunter gatherer, when man and women would consume large amounts, then fast and eat whatever and whenever they could. So, your body needs a continuous variety in what it eats, and how much of it. With that in mind, here are some suggestions for including a wide variety into your nutrition: carbs – brown bread, brown pasta, brown rice, quinoa, and rye crisp breads. Protein – chicken, fish, lamb, beef, tofu, soy, lentils, Quorn and seeds. Fruit – bananas, apples, pears, pineapples, blueberries, raspberries, lemons, tomatoes and blackberries. Vegetables – sweet potatoes, cauliflower, broccoli, cabbage, onions, leeks, beetroot and kale. Good fats – olive oil, almonds, coconut oil and seeds.

10. Diets – Do not diet. Simple. Diets are a quick fix supposed solution that is not sustainable. The weight that you may lose at first will be water weight, and is not a true reflection of your body. Focus on reducing your calories by 20% consistently and don't believe the hype about fruit diets, potato diets and other such nonsense. Your body is designed to require a great variety and depth of vitamins and minerals obtained from a variety of foods, so give it that.

Tip 5 Flexibility

I believe in having both a flexible body and a flexible mind. A flexible body can remind you of what is possible by having a flexible mind, and vice versa. Your body is designed to be naturally flexible, as well as strong and fast. A lot of people I speak to, say that they are not flexible, but this is simply not true. Being flexible is a natural state for the body, we just need to give it the right conditions. Firstly, a lot of tension is held in the hips flexors, glutes and hamstrings; and addressing these areas can massively improve our overall flexibility.

It is also important to set flexibility goals. Being inspired by watching the great success of Nile Wilson and Team GB in the 2016 Olympics in Brazil, I decided I wanted to be able to do the splits. As a child, I could almost do them, but this time, I was determined that I was going to make it happen! So, I searched on YouTube and found a very simple series of stretches, which I copied. After just under two weeks of practising every day for 20 minutes, I could do the splits! And now I can pretty much do them on command. When I get inflexible in my thinking or stuck in an area, I can now drop down into the splits and whilst lying there, I can refocus and keep perspective.

Tip 6 Helping Yourself

It is very important that you see the changes in your eating, fitness and lifestyle as positive ones that will help make you fitter, healthier and happier. They really will. And it is also very important to know when you are empowering yourself, no one is doing it for you – you are truly helping yourself. The way that you look at your lifestyle is very important, so when you are giving the cookies a break for a while, don't think, *Oh I'm depriving myself.* Instead, think that you are now looking after yourself at a higher level. Avoid thinking badly of bad food choices and focus on reminding yourself that you are making good choices and positive changes. This will make all the difference.

Part 2
The Mind

Here you will find tips and suggestions for looking after your mind, which is just as important as the body, if not more so. Again, take what you like, and I'd advise you to remain open minded, be willing to both learn and unlearn and there will be no stopping you!

Inspiration

Inspiration leads to courage, action and success. To be inspired, is to feel alive and is the very best feeling that there is, regardless of which area you experience it in.

Inspiration is my favourite thing about life because it can be experienced anywhere, at any time, by anyone. It's that feeling of wanting to do something great, to really go for it, to achieve, or to share and just to simply be, fully in the moment. There are so many ways to be inspired, but to keep it simple and accessible here are five things that you can do every day. And remember, inspiration ignites your soul!

1   Find inspiring people – search for people either in your own life or famous examples from history, who make you feel good, uplifted and like anything is possible. Read about them, watch videos, see them speak and absorb their energy! Most inspirational people are completely willing to share their resources with you, to show you that you are just as amazing as them and most inspirational stuff is up on the internet for free. Here are some people to get you started. For fitness, try Greg Plitt: a military man turned fitness guru. Also, Scooby: Bodybuilder of 29 years who gives all his ideas away for free! Olympic gold

medallist, Jessica Eniss Hill and the entire GB Olympic and Paralympic teams have been fantastic for our country. For life inspiration, check out Tony Robbins – master communicator, Geoff Thompson – former bouncer turned writer and Rob Moore – a property and financial mastermind. Also, for general incredible inspiration you must simply search about Martin Luther King Jr, Ghandi, The Suffragette Movement and Nick Vujic – an incredible man with no arms and legs.

2   Listen to inspiring podcasts whilst driving, doing the washing or other small menial tasks. Listening to inspiring material whilst doing something boring will not only transform your mood as you do it, but you can do the task whilst also topping up on inspirational material, thereby achieving two goals at once. This is not multi-tasking, but an example of leverage; where one thing can help the other in an interdependent way that doesn't require more work on your behalf.

Examples of recommended podcasts and audio books are:

The Disruptive Entrepreneur by Rob Moore
The Entrepreneur Revolution by Daniel Priestly
Secrets of a Millionaire Mind by T Harv Eker
The TED Radio Hour

3   Reading inspirational phrases or coming up with your own! There are thousands of phrases out there available on the internet that will resonate with you and help you feel inspired. Start by reading them, writing them and looking at them often, then progress to writing your own and repeat them often. Excellent ones to start with include:

"Be the change you want to see." – Ghandi
"Love one another as I have loved you." – Jesus
"Every day above ground is a good day!" – Anon

4   Music – music can lift you and inspire you in seconds in a way that few other things can. Everyone has their own musical tastes and preferences, so pick what you like. But make sure to listen to a wide variety of music for a variety of your moods and situations. You don't necessarily want to be listening to powerful, pumped up '80s' rock all the time. Sometimes, some gentle reggae or layered classical pieces can inspire just as well.

5   Remember your past successes. Stop and think of times when you felt amazing. It might be when you achieved something, or a loving memory with someone. But remember how your body felt, what your thinking was, what it was that made it special for you. And if you can repeat that, go out and make it happen again! If you can't, be grateful for it happening and know you will always have it as a treasured inspired memory.

These people and methods recommended will help you to see that through the power of the human spirit, you really can do anything. Inspiration can fade, so make sure to stay topped up daily by looking at phrases, listening to audio books and podcasts, watching videos and listening to songs. Regularly staying in touch with inspirational material will feed you in a way you won't believe. Also, it is worth pointing out that you yourself may already be an inspirational person to someone else, so embrace that!

Meditation

To sit and be still. To be a human being and not a human doing, will bring you great resources of patience, strength and serenity.

Simply put, meditate: every day. It will relax you, calm your mind, allow you to be awake with an uncluttered mind and enrich your entire life. I have been meditating for about five years properly now and it has transformed my life for the better. There are a variety of ways to do it, and I will begin with a very simple recommendation and method. Visit www.headspace.com and sign up to their *Take 10* programme. It is a totally free programme where you meditate ten minutes a day for ten days. You can also get the Headspace app, which I use, to enable you to meditate anywhere. A man called Andy, who is a trained monk, leads the practice; with a calm and serene countenance that immediately puts you at ease.

You sit still and begin with some deep breathing, then close your eyes and follow his instructions as he leads you through a body scan and deeper into a basic meditation practice. You can watch a variety of excellent videos that explain the concepts and Andy has given many talks on the subject, which are easy to find online.

I found that when I meditate, I give my mind some time to just 'be'. Even when we are asleep, our bodies and minds are sorting through the day's events, thoughts and experiences – deleting bits, restructuring others, filling things away; it never really stops. But with meditation, it stops. Quite quickly. And it is common to sit at the end of a meditation practise and simply think nothing at all for several seconds: sit still, with a calm, blank mind, at ease and resting in the present moment. Try it out, you will be amazed at the results.

Prayer

To be aware of the other problem, situation or place. To reach out beyond one's self can enrich everything.

To me, prayer is a chance to stop, reflect, to give thanks and be grateful for life and to look beyond ourselves to something greater. For some that means to a god or gods, to others it is more of an appreciation of our universe and its incredible complexity and vastness. I do not think those parts matter as much as the actual practice. For me, I love to take the time to be grateful for my life, to count the many incredible things and experiences and have moments of solidarity with those who are suffering and think, *"What can I do in my own life to help others?"*

If you find the idea of the word 'prayer' uncomfortable, simply call it quiet time. I begin, always, by reflecting on how fortunate we are to be here: the odds of us being born at all are over 1 in 13 trillion! So, if you are reading this, know that you are already incredibly fortunate. I'd also take the time to consider the beauty of nature, the possibility of the human spirit and all the good things in your life. You can also consider suffering, pain and the worst things of life. But one is not more powerful and they do not cancel out each other, like hot and cold make lukewarm. Instead, you can consider both these aspects, as they are both parts of life. You can live in solidarity with the poor, through supporting them financially and emotionally, as well as fully living the joy and happiness of your own life. So, take some quiet time, enrich that part of you that you can't quite touch, and enjoy.

The Whole

All should be done according to the whole.

That is the way I consider the mind and the body and that has been the aim of this section of the book. I see a lot of examples of fixed, closed minds today: people saying their body and their mind are one certain way, or their health and happiness depends on someone or something else. I believe that to declare such things is to disempower yourself. Yes, there are powerful, incredible life experiences, situations and people that can shake us both beautifully and terribly. But ultimately, if you possess the mental and physical means to take on this subject of living well in a respectful and meaningful way, you are sitting on a mound of gold! Your ability to choose where you go and what you believe means that you are your own best resource; you are your own answers and those that you do not have, yet are already being shared with lots of love by others. So, be courageous! Live your life as one whole entity, not a variety of conflicting subplots and bits. Look at it as one thing – your life. And know that it is a precious one, a beautiful one and by living it fully and according to the whole, it will be spectacular.

Part 3
Spiritual Serenity

Guidelines for a Wholistic, Happy Spirit

Where Will Your Spirit Lead You?

Introduction

This section of the book will explore the spirit, the energy and the life force of your life. It will use examples from modern life, history, my own experience and that of several cultures to demonstrate this. As the body and mind work together, the spirit wraps them up tight and holds you strong and full of energy, like a super charged Christmas present!

Your own spirit and that of others, as well as the issue of spirituality and more global spiritual issues are fascinating and beautiful areas to explore, when living a reflective, meaningful life, lived according to the whole.

Let your spirit bloom

Training Your Spirit

I am going to share with you three ways that will allow you to train your spirit by linking it with your body and mind into one cohesive whole.

1 Cold exposure

I have recently been learning about the power of cold exposure in the human spirit. Firstly, look up Wim Hoff, an incredible Dutch man, who turned the tragedy of his wife's suicide into a driving force of love for humanity: http://www.wimhofmethod.com

He advocates cold showers and cold exposure as a way of training your body, mind, and spirit. I now have cold showers daily and they really do revitalise you. You can also try ice baths or showers which alternate hot and cold and walks out in cold conditions. Be careful however, to be sensible and look after your general health by seeing your doctor first.

2   Breathing

Your breathing is the most fundamentally important thing that you can do to align yourself in body, mind and spirit. There are many different breathing practises and techniques and I am going to focus on two which you can start using safely straight away. By controlling your breath, it helps to control and stabilise both your body and mind, which can lead to a feeling of becoming more aware of your spirit.

Firstly, the seated version. Sit up with your shoulders down and back and make sure you are sitting upright with good posture. You can sit in a chair or cross legged on the floor. Focus gently on a spot straight in front of you. Breathe in deeply to a count of three, and breathe out for a count of six. Repeat these ten times. For standing, stand upright with shoulders down and back and good posture. Bend your knees slightly and keep a nice wide stance and look slightly upwards. Perform the same breathing as the seated version. We generally breathe too shallowly and by slowing down our breathing, we allow our body and mind to synchronise and relax, which provides the space for our spirit to be nourished in silence and stillness.

The second breathing technique is to be used to generate some energy into your spirit, and is useful if you have been sitting down for a long time. It will help to revitalise you. Begin by adopting the same seated or standing posture as before. Then breathe in deeply from your belly for four seconds and out for two. Repeat ten times. By breathing in more than breathing out, you are getting lots of oxygen into your system and lowering your CO_2 levels, which will help you to really feel the energy generated – which is the energy used – vital and light, perfect for nourishing your spirit.

3 Space

The third thing is a technique I call **The Space Technique**. Its focus is to create more space in your mind and thus to grow the strength of your spirit. The practice is very simple and its effects are profound. You can do it in two ways: outside in the world or inside in your mind. To do it outside, simply step outside your house and find an open space, preferably where you can see a clear sky. Look at the space around, the expansiveness, the space in between objects, there is nothing squashed together at all. Feel the peace of knowing this. No matter how busy or stressed your life is, there is always an infinite space between things. Even on a subatomic level, each atom is made up or primarily empty space. Beyond our planet lie vast distances of empty space. It is the natural order of things.

If you do not have access to a large, open space, *google image search* one in your phone and close your eyes and visualise one, or use one from memory. The effect will be the same. By focusing on the vast space between things, your mind calms and so does your spirit. It is like feeding your spirit; each time you focus on space, balance, health, wholeness, solidarity, kindness, such focus feeds your spirits and helps it to growth in stature.

Let your spirit flow

Unstoppable Spirit

When you are 'in the zone', when 'your spirits are high', when you 'feel inspired'; there are phrases that are used to try and express the experience of having an unstoppable spirit: **in the zone, energised, in the flow, at one with things**. These phrases aim to try and convey that which we cannot see and yet feel so strongly in those moments – our spirit. Once a person sets their spirit upon something, there is no force that can stop them. It is challenging to create this state at will. However, there are things that you can do to increase the regularity of these moments. Here are two of the most powerful examples of actions you can take to create and sustain such an unstoppable spirit.

Align your life with your values – what you feel passionately about.

Whenever your actions and consequences move you away from your true values, it will drain your spiritual energy levels. However, by performing actions and deeds in your work place, with loved ones and in everyday life, which are in line with your values, your spirit will feel nourished. There will be no conflict between what you think, say and feel and what you do. You will be acting from a place deep inside you, which you know is right and true.

Give to others – feel the needs of others within yourself.

When we give to others, we reach beyond ourselves, towards something else. We manage to put someone or something beyond ourselves and this can have a profound effect upon our spirits. Some of the greatest examples in history of the power of the human spirit, Martin Luther King Junior's Civil rights movement to name just one, have come from people aligning themselves together towards a cause greater than themselves, to a belief, to a *dream*.

Channel the darkness of your spirit

Negative Energy Spirit

Once I was doing some hill-running training, which is extremely tough: you run as fast as you can up a hill and then jog back down and repeat. It is an excellent form of physical training and it is also very gruelling. This hill reached up, then plateaued and reached again three more times – I called it *The Dragon*. On this day, I was struggling. Usually, I focused on positive thoughts or physical sensations such as my breathing to power me up the hill. But no matter how much I tried, horrible thoughts of death, violence, destruction and panic kept filling my mind and my body was responding very sluggishly. But on this day, as I bumbled down the hill, I had an idea. This time as I scaled the hill, I would not stop the negative thoughts and sensations, I would welcome them. I figured this couldn't result in me feeling any worse, so I could at least try it. The results were incredible.

As the painful thoughts came, I said inside my mind, *Yes welcome! What else have you got for me?* and I sped up. They kept coming and I kept welcoming them, I felt pain, fear, sadness; all terrible things in those thirty or so seconds, but the difference was, I was using them as fuel. I powered up the hill faster than I ever had before and as I stood hunched over with my hands on my knees, panting heavily I thought, *what has just happened here?*

What had happened was, that I had harnessed the power of my darker spiritual moments. If I was the fire, I had used any old rubbish and thrown it on, and regardless of what it was, it had caught alight and burnt strongly and fed the fire inside. This realisation was revolutionary in how I approached myself, my thinking and the effects of my thoughts and feelings on my spirit. This story can be very helpful in how we look at what can nourish us and what can destroy us. As Geoff Thompson says,

"We are the alchemists of our life."
https://www.amazon.co.uk/Geoff-
Thompson/e/B005X6P6VE

This means that no matter what ingredients life gives us: thoughts, experiences, beliefs, people, we can transform how we look at them just by believing that we can, and make them work for us. Hence, being ill can be an opportunity for reading, horrible thoughts can help us think more laterally, everything can nourish the spirit, if we can perceive that it can. Just as all of us are provided with life and sustained through light and water, the spirit can be fed, grown and nourished by both the positive and the negative as well, we do not need to just close ourselves off to one aspect.

Everything can nourish your spirit

Aligning Your Spirit

The ultimate spirit is the energy of life: the interconnectedness that links us all. Regardless of spiritual, cultural, or political beliefs, we are all made of the same materials and occupy a universe made up of the same things we can see, and most which we cannot. Your spirit does not have a culture, language, class, or religion, although you may ascribe to one or several of these. It is my experience that by travelling to other countries and speaking other languages, you open yourself up beyond your previous boundaries. Similarly, by experiencing and understanding different cultures, religions, and political systems, one can increase the circumference of their spirit without diluting its contents into a mush of different things.

One good example of this was a trip I made to Romania. I learned basic Romanian phrases and was keen to speak and practise with its people. My host in one city, Sergu, asked if I would like to come out with him and his friends into town.

There were no English speakers except Sergu and me and that did not matter one bit to me. His Russian friend, Radu, spoke good Romanian and I will never forget him rapping Eminem lyrics as we walked down the street home. He could recite the lyrics to *Cleaning out my Closet* in perfect English without understanding a word of it. He would finish the song and look at me, and I was astounded he could speak such good English without understanding their meaning. And then it hit me. Here was a Romanian, an Englishman and a Russian, able to speak to each other through the shared language of Romanian. If I had not been willing to speak the language and open myself up beyond my comfortable limits, I would not have met such wonderful people and had such brilliant times.

This example shows the capacity of our spirits to transcend cultural and language boundaries and find common ground together. There is something which unites us beyond our words, our actions and even our bodies: something beyond all which we make our home in. By being willing to stretch out boundaries and reach out into the unknown, our spirits widen their circumference, we become capable of so much more and we open to so many more possibilities because of this.

This wonderful experience in Romania and this realisation has led to further adventures in Greece, Turkey, Scotland, Malta, Egypt and Czech Republic. In fact, these flexible principles resulted in me, recently, giving mental coaching to a former top champion table tennis player in Czech. He had all the physical skills and yet saw something in me, which he wanted to apply to his game, to improve his mindset. I happily obliged and used a mixture of basic Czech phrases, lots of hand gestures and much enthusiasm. As we laughed and hugged after 20 minutes of excited chatter, I knew that my spirit was one for universal adaptability and was open and willing to give to all.

You too possess the same spirit, and can access such moments – you simply need to be willing to embrace its universality. You are far more than your nationality: you are a person of the world and by embracing that you will open yourself up to experiences wider and deeper than you thought possible.

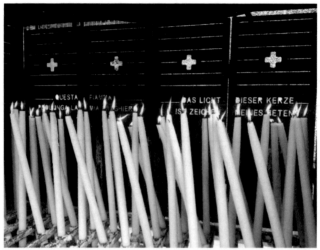

Let your spirit burn bright day and night

Accessing 'The Universal Spirit'

Our world is a wonderful, magical one full of energies and forces, many of which we can feel but not see or quite put our finger on. I believe that this is a fantastic thing. I would not want life to be always measurable, predictable, isolated, sterile, and quaint. And yet, embracing life as a sprawling interconnected river presents challenges chiefly, how to keep our heads above water and not sink to the bottom.

Firstly, just by being here we all have access to what I would call, *The Universal Spirit*. Let me define what I mean by this. Each person is full of the spirit of life, the fire inside, the joy beyond our bones. And it is not just people who possess this. All living things are filled and brought to life by this energy, this wonderful life force, this spirit. Scientists would refer to it as energy and focus on the forces and matter which interact to create and shape our world. Religious people would point to a god or gods, who move, shape and live in us. And so, both pay testaments in different ways to what I call

47

The Universal Spirit *– the force of life*. It is in all of us, and simply by being alive you have access to this incredible phenomenon. I would like to recommend some ways in which you can reconnect and become aware and conscious of this beautiful fact.

Spending time in nature nourishes your soul. Walking under the trees, smelling fresh air, squinting in the sun, and catching glimpses of the various animals that live alongside us, will remind you that we live in *nature*, it is our natural way. Yes, we have towns, cities and civilisations, and yet the natural, the rural, anything not man-made pulls us, calls to us, and wants us to be near. I would suggest daily quiet, slow walks outside where you simply watch, listen, and learn from this incredible living, beautiful landscape and its creatures.

As well as taking time to be in and around nature, I would also advocate taking time to just be. We have become human doings, and it is imperative that we spend time daily as human beings. This could take the form of formal meditation or prayer, or simply sitting quietly with a cup of tea for five minutes. The point of it is to get out of your own way, to quieten your mind and all distractions enough to allow your spirit to come forth, to tell you how you really are, on a level deeper than your thoughts and feelings. You may discover there is an issue you need to address within yourself, or that you are far happier than you thought you were. These realisations of the spirit all come from an ability to sit and be at peace with yourself. I'd recommend this is done daily: begin with five minutes, and as you become more comfortable, build up from there.

This leads on to another important way to align with the universal spirit: solitude. The paradox of being human is that we feel the need to be with others and yet also, we feel the deep pull to spend time alone. Although we have family, friends and loved ones all around us, when we die, we will pass beyond on them, and do so alone. To embrace this fact of dying alone is not morbid or alienating, it allows us to be close to ourselves as well as with others. Make time to be with just yourself, and see what happens. Embrace the fact that there is only one you, celebrate this; get to know yourself better and your spirit will grow, become stronger and you will also be more comfortable with others because you will recognise that you do not need anyone else. You are free to do both, be with others and be alone, you are free in spirit to simply be.

Having said that, some of the most fulfilling and happy times of the spirit can come when we are with others. The river of life includes all people and embracing this interconnectedness can bring an appreciation and empathy and deep love for one another that is rooted naturally in our very being.

I will often marvel at how time with my loved ones allows me to go beyond myself, to be part of something communal, to grow relationships and to be part of something special. Music, sport and art, all these wonderful human expressions are a testament to the spirit reaching out to share with others. Here is a simple analogy to remember how our spirits can come together. Imagine a sporting or musical event in a huge stadium you have seen or been to. Remember the sounds, the powerful feelings of anticipation and energy, excitement and power. Remember how loud it was, the movement of the crowd and the shared experience you had with others. Now imagine that same stadium with only you and the performer in it. Not quite the same, is it? And so, it is with life; some of our best moments will be through shared spirits coming together and celebrating experiences.

Another way to align yourself with the universal spirit is to embrace challenge, struggle and difficulty. To continue with the river metaphor, a river can rage and crash and sometimes it must climb up hill. The moments where you feel you cannot cope, are where your spirit can shine. You are so much more powerful and capable than you think you are. There are many stories of parents lifting cars to rescue children or people surviving in the most terrible conditions. What do these examples tell us? That the human spirit is one of the greatest forces in this world! It is often in such extreme situations that we can recognise and appreciate this, and yet, our spirits are incredible and wonderful in even the most mundane of days. Simply knowing that there are no limits to the power and energy of your spirit can be vastly uplifting. Your spiritual resources are not like a bucket with liquid in and once they are used up they are gone. No, your spirit is much more like the grains of sand in all of earth's beaches, the number of stars in the sky, the depth of a parents' love, and the vast distances of space. There is no end to your spirit and so know this daily, your spirit is incredible and there to help you every day. Take time to nourish your spirit, to care for yourself and you will have access to this most incredible life force always. Know and believe that every single human spirit is more powerful than all the computers, machines and man-made mechanisms put together in the history of time. What an awe-inspiring thought that the river of life, the universal spirit, is unlimited in its resources, and so are you.

Take a moment to be silent and recognise this. Take a moment to appreciate how utterly amazing life is, and you are. Take a moment to be thankful for this wondrous, beautiful force that surrounds you, cares for you, nourishes you and lives both within and beyond you. Your spirit is the very essence of you, your purest and most powerful form and through taking the time daily to appreciate it and nourish it, it will care and love for you. Taking one step further and recognising that your spirit can be aligned with a universal one will bring you peace, serenity and an inner glow which you simply cannot get from anywhere else. Your spirit belongs to an ancient yet brand new, vital energy and it will sustain and love you throughout all your years.

Where is your spirit leading you now?

Your spirit is a wonderful thing: it reaches beyond your earthly limits and brings you into contact with the possibilities of abundance and transcendence, which can offer any of our happiest and most fulfilling life experiences. I hope and wish you a happy life lived in the spirit, full of joy and serenity:

May your spirit rise and soar
Lifting you up beyond the worries of the day
May your spirit plunge
Into the depths of your being to renew you every way
May your spirit protect you

With a million beautiful rays of light
And may your spirit hold you close
As any loved one or friend might

May your spirit lift you every day

Part 4
Digital Health

We now live in a digital world: one of broadband, fibre optics optic connections, Wi-Fi, drones, artificial intelligence, Google, all sorts of fascinating and fantastic digital creations. And this has a massive influence on our health. Our iPhone or Android phones that we carry around in our pockets have more influence and interactions with us than anything else during a day. Often there is a lag in cultures catching up with the latest technology and its subsequent effects on our behaviour, but the speed is now becoming so fast that it is imperative that we become more focused and proactive regarding our presence in this digital world. For if we do not, we run the risk of becoming displaced and left out by the very technology that has been invented to help enrich our lives.

We now need to examine our digital health, which I believe is a vitally important part of the consideration of wholistic health for the modern day human being. As well as the body, mind, spirit and heart, we now have a digital aspect which we interact, perform and practise with every day in our lives, whether we realise it or not. I will begin to introduce this concept to you by relating it to other aspects of health, to keep the concept relevant and applicable to daily life. Firstly, we must consider what our digital diet is, *what information are you taking in daily?* Is it useful, quality information that will enhance your life and health or is it junk like pornography, fake news, uninformed opinions, gambling and downright rubbish? Whatever you choose to ingest, and process daily will be having a massive impact on your health either way.

A useful way of looking at our digital health is to consider our online presence as a character, an avatar. The more information you put online, the more complex and full this avatar becomes. However, a word of caution: in the digital world, it is easy to be anonymous, false and to exaggerate our strengths and underplay our weaknesses. We must always retain a degree of healthy scepticism and safety when dealing with people online, as one would on the street with a stranger. So, as well as considering that you have an online character, it is also important to consider your position and your poise in relation to your health. Whatever you post and interact with online will influence others, just as in the world outside. So, someone who donates money to worthy causes, writes an informative and useful blog and volunteers for the online Samaritans page, will have a very different impact on the world to someone who gambles online, watches hardcore pornography, surfs the dark web and engages in trolling and abusing others anonymously via social media.

As with anything, there is no judgement implied here, I am pointing out the differences in cause and effect, due to human choice and interaction with others, as we have with everything. So, how does one go about being digitally healthy, happy, productive and flourishing? As with every aspect of health, it is important to first understand where we are to begin with, where we would like to go and then consider how we are going to get there. Let's begin.

1. Begin with an audit – keep a digital diary for a week regarding how long you are online each day and when you have time off. What categories your online time goes into: education, recreation, information, entertainment, shopping, boredom, sexual or communicative.

Let's start with an audit about you. Write down all the ways that you can think of where you interact with the digital world – through tablets, phones, laptops, computers, drones, TVs, everything. Consider the following:
Which devices do you use?
How much time do you spend on them during an average day? On weekends?

How much does that add up to overall in a week?
What do you use the internet and digital devices for?

Some suggestions include: for entertainment, for communication, for information, for fun, for research, for self-development, for escape, for emotional reasons, for health reasons, for financial reasons, for sexual reasons, for shopping.

Now you will know:

1. Which devices you use.
2   For how long.
3   What you engage in the digital world for.

Now let's use that information to begin to classify it.

2   Ideas for improving digital health include: a digital detox, no screen or phone time for a time. Also, creating some social norms for yourself around technology. For example, occasionally going out without your phone or keeping certain times as important and without phones, such as dinner time and time in nature.

It is important that we recognise that creating dichotomies is of limited use. So, saying things like, I will spend the day without my phone, whilst admirable, is only step one. The first thing I'd recommend instead is to know the numbers for how much time you spend on your phone and devices, which situations you use them in, which you don't and looking at that. Then, it is helpful to think about *effectiveness*. There have been several excellent books written on how to be more productive in business and life using less time and understanding concepts such as leverage. I'd like to pick up from a slightly different place.

Firstly, I believe that we as people spend too much time on our phones. I also believe that most of the time we spend using our phones, devices and the internet, is generally spent on shallow things such as shopping, entertainment and gossiping. Now, I am not suggesting a moral superiority, far from it. Instead I'd like to use the excellent concept or *marginal gains* to suggest improvements. For example, if you improve your sales conversions by just 10%, then your profits margins will increase dramatically. Let us think in the same way. What if we spent 10% of our online, digital time as an investment – in our education, health, community, finances, spirituality? Consider the benefit of five hours a week extra time spent on personal development, community work, spiritual practices, reaching out to others. We are spending this time in a passive non-profitable way. Why not invest some of our time, which we would spend anyway, on ourselves and others? I am not advocating that we do not use our digital devices. On the contrary, I am advocating a full and robust use of them for exactly the purposes they were created for – to make things more accessible, connectable and manageable so we can profit from that and perform great deeds and live wonderful lives. We now have a digital aspect to our lives; the digital aspect should not have us.

3   Ideas to improve your digital health – putting positivity into the online world, making healthy choices, thinking long term – like with food choices. Exercising and improving your skills: it will help you both professionally and personally as the internet and technology will continue to play a larger and more integrated role in our lives.

Let's explore some of the ways in which we can begin doing this today.

Putting Out Positivity

It is always worth taking the time to consider the meaning and content of what you say online. As unlike the world outside, where conversations and events can be forgotten or misconstrued; online, there is a permanent visible file of everything you post. And I feel it is also worth pointing out that the recipients of anything negative or abusive posts online are not machines, but real people full of emotions and feelings. Once you put something up there that is negative or hurtful, it is contributing to ongoing problems, difficulties, and it is not doing any good to anyone. I fully believe one should be able to critique, criticise and offer opinions; however, once they stray into the painful and hurtful, there is no need for them.

Let us not focus on not doing negative things, rather we should focus on and promote the wonderful, incredibly positive possibilities that come with our limitless digital age. We can now send messages of love and support to other sides of the world, which are received in seconds. We can share photos, videos, inspirational and uplifting content. And if what we want to see is not up there yet, we can create it ourselves and upload it to a worldwide audience. It is now more straightforward and accessible than ever to find information, to connect with others and to, as Ghandi said, *be the change that you want to see.*

Making Healthy Choices

Thinking long-term – when we can consider long period of time and events and situations over long periods of times, such as years, it can give us good perspective. Firstly, consider what you are doing and saying digitally: is it making a positive contribution over time? Is it building something? Another benefit of thinking long term is that it allows us to think in terms of building things, in terms of scale, of doing great things, and ultimately, of legacy. I try to make sure that my digital output reflects who I am as a person, my vision and values and contributes towards my dreams, my goals and what I want to build over the coming decades.

Helping Others

I believe that as one united human family we have a duty towards helping others. It runs so intrinsically deep as part of ourselves to share, to empathise, to love and to care for each other. A parents' love, a strong friendship, a robust partnership, a dynamic work team, there are so many examples of us reaching out towards others, I believe this should be reflected in our digital practises. We are living in an unprecedentedly powerful time in human history, where the average person can make a meaningful and strong impact on global issues in a remarkably short space of time. Thanks to broadband, crowdsourcing, the internet and instant messaging. I feel it is important to always consider the other person when posting online and when taking part in digital practises – they cannot ultimately be a purely selfish act. There are many aspects which, although were first considered individual, could be opportunities to help others. Buying and shopping can be linked quite easily to donating an extra portion to a local homeless charity. Clothes which are sent back and partially damaged can be recycled and distrusted at very little cost to companies. Free education on thousands of topics can and is being uploaded onto YouTube daily – a digital video platform which is offering this for free. If you contributed towards these efforts you could improve the health of others with minimal money needed and have both a local and global positive impact.

Thinking and Acting BIG

We live in a paradox of a world that is huge in terms of size, yet we can traverse it in seconds through digital devices. It is a world of global small businesses that can be very small in terms of team size (two to ten people) and generate billions in value – think of Airbnb, Uber, Instagram and WhatsApp for recent examples. So, I believe that we should be consistently thinking and acting BIG. After all, we have one life on one planet, which is tiny in the vast cosmic web, so any perspectives we have on size and what is large are all subjectively relevant anyway.

So, how can we think and act BIG digitally? Here's a few suggestions:

1. *Think in terms of 100 years*. If you could be guaranteed to live to 100 years of age, what would you be building, creating, contributing towards now?

Having this freedom of lots of time allows us the space to think more timelessly, to pace ourselves and not feel rushed.

2. *Use Fear* – this is an interesting one. I hear a lot about using fear as your friend and motivating yourself to do things that scare you. But I'd like to suggest something slightly different. I have used the internet throughout the years to learn as much as I can about things that scare me, to educate myself to understand them more; from animals to places, people to concepts. By having more information, you are in a better position to make an informed decision, opinion or judgement on something. And it can create some surprising results. I learnt so much about sharks that this year I swam with some and loved it. Now I am planning to do a cage dive with Great Whites. This digital trail of enquiry may well surprise and delight you.

3. *Consider Purpose* – are you pursuing your purpose digitally, as well as spiritually? I think it is good to consider what you are contributing towards digitally, and to what purpose. Are you just seeking entertainment, gratification, or something more meaningful? Have a look at your scores from earlier on in this chapter to reassess how your online presence is tying in with your purpose, vision and values.

4. *Love* – putting more love out there is always a good thing. From sharing photos with family members, to using Amazon, 1 click delivery to surprise loved ones with gifts, to taking the time to FaceTime or chat, putting love out into the digital world will help us as humans to maintain our humanity in all our artistic and technological expressions. We are not merely logical, and the artistic, creative, loving side of humanity must also have a place full and vibrant part in our digital world.

Bringing It All Together

We are aiming here to optimise your digital health – where can you go? What are some ideals to strive towards? In order to understand this let us ask the great aged questions of: *Where are you? Where have you come from? Where are you going?* As they relate to digital health, they provide wonderfully compelling and exciting possibilities.

Where Are We? Where Are You?

We are now living in a world of fibre optic broadband that travels faster than the speed of light. With quantum computers available and being used every day, we have now transcended the old problem areas of speed and size to a large extent. The size and speed of a natural object does not equate to its digital size and form. This has wonderful implications for storage of data. We are now in a world where more people are connected onto the internet than ever before. However, there are still many billions that are illiterate, unconnected, homeless and in pain. So, there is still much work to be done. It is important that we do not wash over such issues and pretend that they are not happening. However, with falling prices and speeding advances, it is true that high quality technology, internet access and digital devices are more accessible than ever before. Where do you fit into all of this? Are you excited by it and the coming future? Are you scared? Are you possibly feeling a bit of both? Take some time to consider where you feel you are in this digital world, and where you would like to be. For example, would you like to learn some new skills? Lose old habitual ways of thinking? Connect with more people? Produce more digitally rather than just consuming? Think of where you are right now and where you would like to go.

Where Have We Come From? Where Have You Come From?

We have come from a place where computers in their current forms did not even exist 100 years ago. The growth of the digital world has been completely exponential. Distances used to take days, weeks, and months to travel; now they take nanoseconds. Size and weight of objects used to be so important, now they can be sent weightlessly through email and the cloud. It is so important that we understand the way things are today in the digital world, because the changes are so incredibly recent for many of the people on the planet that it is an ongoing shock and a challenge to engage with. We must take the time and make the effort to make sure that those who come from a time before, are able to interact and thrive in this world, alongside those of us who love it. *Our technology is for the whole of mankind, not just the quick, or the young or the able bodied.* Where have you come from digitally? Have you always had computers? When did you first get a mobile phone? How long have you had the current habits and practices that you now employ every day? It is useful to pause and consider these questions.

Where Are We Going? Where Are You Going?

So, where are we going? There are definite trends and patterns, as well as possibilities which we can consider. Firstly, the internet and digital world is now here to stay, and so will continue to influence and drive change. The speed and efficiency of machines, the internet, quantum computers, artificial intelligence, phones, tablets, cars, all digital devices, as well as those attached to them, will become more efficient, more connected and it seems, more centralised. This has some fascinating and beautiful ramifications for us as a species. Illnesses, disease and pain will now be subject to more rigorous and detailed analysis and potential cures. Structurally, the less and less we need to rely on physical machines, the more space both physically and digitally, we will be able to occupy. Space now seems to be back on the cards for the adventurous to explore.

The most exciting development for me personally comes from the currently incomplete scientific world we now live in through Quantum Mechanics. We understand some of how things interact and exist, but utilising digital technology will allow us to continue to transcend our size and physical bodies to delve into both the micro and the macro in currently incomprehensible ways. The challenge for us, as humanity is to make sure that we continue to evolve alongside our technology: to empathise, to strive, to feel, to suffer, to live out the experience of life to its full alongside, not just via, our digital world.

Part 5
The Heart

Ten Wonderful Gifts Your Heart Will Give to You

The best works are done from the heart. They come from deep within. They are selfless, kind, full of vitality, energy and power. There are so many wonderful people out in our world living from the heart and that makes me happy. I admire all those who serve others and themselves with a joyful heart, this world is a place of endless renewal. This is from my heart to theirs and to yours.

1. Kindness

Being kind is such an important part of life. Kindness is soft and pliable and gentle. Being kind allows us to act for others, to think well of them, to support them. Kindness helps us to accept ourselves just as we are right now. Kind words, thoughts and actions will always steer us towards and into a great place. Kindness saves. Kind acts create bridges, heal hurts and help us to look beyond ourselves to something more interdependent. A kind word, smile or action will do nothing but good if done with the right intentions. Being kind towards others also helps us to be kind to ourselves.

A Story of Kindness

I recently read a book which encouraged me to do more kind acts. I got into a disagreement with someone, who suggested that as I was planning my acts of 'kindness', my intentions were therefore not genuine. However, I disagreed. By doing my kind acts deliberately, I built up the habit of kindness, and so began to look out for opportunities to be kind randomly and whenever I could. My acts included baking fruit loafs for neighbours, smiling at people, lending money and offering advice. I suggest you try it!

Kindness Opportunity

Identify some actions that you could take to be kind towards others in your life. They could be family, friends, work colleagues or strangers. They only need to be small things to start with: smiles, hugs, kind words, and thinking kind thoughts towards others. These kind aspects will help you to step outside of yourself and direct your heart and all its wonderful goodness towards others.

To be kind is to see the other as a part of you, an extension of your own heart, only separated by bodies. To be kind is to embrace the beautiful diversity of the world and its people and to choose to add, to contribute to it in a meaningful way. It takes no thought to be cruel and yet to be kind is such a privilege, and to do it is free. Do not underestimate the value of this free wonder in the lives and eyes of others.

2. Patience

Patience is one of the most important qualities that you can grow, possess, craft and treasure in your life. Every single day requires patience. Every situation requires moments of patience. Patience is ever needed and yet, never seemingly sought. I used to work with children and was always asked:

"How do you have the patience for that?! I would not have the patience for it!"

These people I spoke with seemed to think that their patience was a limited amount, like a liquid in a bucket. And once it was used up, it was gone. However, I'd like to suggest an alternative image, which has helped me in difficult times, that of an elastic band. Your patience is like an elastic band: it will stretch and stretch and just when you think that it is going to snap, it can stretch a little more, and then return to its starting point. I rarely found that I snapped, instead I stretched and stretched and only became more flexible. Like love, inside the heart is the potential for endless patience.

A Story of Patience

I worked as a primary school teacher for several years, and that required a great deal of patience every day. I remember one day seeing a child sitting on the carpet, trying to upset others. I told the other children to ignore that child, I moved other children, and I carried on reading the story. I did not make eye contact, I could feel that I had the opportunity to be annoyed, however, I continued as I was and eventually the child got bored, although it did take 20 minutes. Another time I found out one of my children had been fighting and had really hurt another child. This initially upset me and I could feel that I could have acted in an annoyed or angry way. Instead, I chose to turn it into a learning experience for all of us.

I stood up in front of the class, explained what had happened and told the children that I was upset; I asked them if they could understand why and they said they could. Then I said, "Watch this," and I took a deep breath and physically calmed myself down. I did this several times and they could see my body relaxing and my face beginning to smile. I asked the children and they agreed that if I could do it, they could do the same.

Patience Opportunity

The next time you are in a situation that requires patience, remember that it is both a lifetime skill and an infinite resource. Try laughing, thinking creatively and thinking BIG to help you shift your perspective. Try this with people who do not have much patience and see if you can help them.

3. Forgiveness

How far can forgiveness go? What happens when you forgive someone? Do you regain power back for yourself which they took from you? No, you transcend such trivial ways of thinking. You step outside the picture and you can see it with new eyes. You look with the eyes of love and see a fellow, flawed human being and love them and yourselves regardless. When you forgive yourself, you open a door in a crowded room in your heart; you open a window, you can even leave the house of shame. Do not limit yourself. Never hold grudges against yourself, it will figuratively kill you from the inside. Instead, forgive and forgive often, in little ways, so it becomes a habit, a brilliant useful everyday habit, like brushing your teeth. Grudges only look backward, forgiveness creates a way forward.

A Story of Forgiveness

I was very hurt by a friend. I found out that they had been lying to me for a long time and it hurt. I felt foolish and confused, but holding onto my pain caused by the situation, only hurt me. What I did to solve it was to forgive the person in my heart, even though I never actually saw them again. What that did, was to remind me that it was not what they did that hurt me; it was how I saw it, my feelings, my own thoughts that upset me. And I could change and control these. After I forgave the person and stopped indulging in feelings of anger, resentment and bitterness I found that the issue did not upset me at all. I wished him well in his life and although, I never saw him again, I was not unhappy about this as I was no longer upset.

Forgiveness Opportunity

Who do you need to forgive in your life now? Is it someone else or even yourself? Is it something from long ago or something more recent? If you can speak with the person, try and do so. And if not, forgive them in your heart and in your mind and move on. Do not indulge in replaying the event and getting hurt over and over again, as once you have chosen to forgive someone, to continue in this negative vein and be selfish is unhelpful to anyone. Once you have forgiven, be proud of yourself! It's a great thing to have achieved. You will have let go of a major hindrance in your life and you will have more energy for the good in your life.

4. Generosity

How generous are you? How generous is your family? How generous are we as one human family? Do we see ourselves in this way? If not, how do we measure our generosity? To me, to be generous means to go further than expected, to lift someone up higher and higher, to consider and to sacrifice for someone or for the greater good.

The world has been so generous to you in giving your life: a body, family, friends, nature, music, food, the air that you breathe. The entire gift of life is an expression of generosity, and so it is a large part of the natural order of things. Parents love and give to the next generation, the best gifts are those shared and to be generous is to realise that an abundance is always possible, not a lack. This does not just mean time and money. Think of how many breathes of air you took today. Could you guess how many there were? Did you have to pay for them? Work for them? Earn them? No, they were freely given to you in a spirit of generosity and abundance that is possible in all areas of life.

The fantastic thing about generosity is, like all the gifts of the heart, it can easily be a way of life for us, lived day by day. All it takes is some consideration and willingness to help. Have a look around – can you give time, affection, consideration and love to someone or something else? I'm sure you can! There's no limit on how generous you can be if you remember that the world is an abundant place, and to give to another will never diminish you as the gifts from the heart never run dry. Generosity of spirit is one of the best things which you can offer to someone, as it demonstrates to others and to yourself that you do not believe in limitations and that being helping and doing for others is as much the natural way as the trees growing roots in the soil of the earth.

A Story of Generosity

To be generous is a part life. Giving gifts, sharing experiences and helping others can be a daily thing. I knew a man who, despite not having much money or time to spare, always made the effort to buy presents and spend time with others. He did this for the entire time I knew him for over 30 years until he died. To offer to others, is to realise and celebrate the reality of life's abundance: it is not a finite resource. It is all in how we see it. And in giving to others and putting them first, we proclaim that we will not subsequently go without. We will be fine, we will be safe and we will grow in confidence to be more generous.

Generosity Opportunity

Do you believe that you have limited time, money and resources? Could you put the needs of another in front of your own to challenge this? Try doing so, and see what the results are for you.

5. Giving

Give yourself away you got yourself for free anyway!

Our bodies, our families, all the beauty and wonder of life have all come to us for free. And so, giving is, therefore, an essential part of the natural order of things. We even die to make way for future generations and so, even our death becomes a selfless, if perhaps an involuntary act. Give! Just because it is a good thing to do.

I have given gifts, I have bought and passed on items but the most profound moments of giving have been where I have given my time and my very best self. Whether that be spending an extra 20 minutes at the side of a dying friend on his final day, working as a primary school teacher giving my absolute best to the children in my care, or even just listening to someone without focusing on what I was going to say next. The very best gift that you can give is yourself. You are so special and to so many people, simply spending time with you is a beautiful blessing to them. Acknowledge that this is not something to boast about but as a testament to how important we all are to each other.

A Story of Giving

There was a teacher who thought that a pupil of his was fantastic. When the teacher left the school, the child gave him his favourite object in the world: his favourite football card, and cried and cried because he was going to miss him so much. In all his years of teaching that card meant so much to him, because he knew the value of it. Until that day, the child had said he would never sell or swop the card as it was priceless. He would keep it forever. And yet he gave it away...

The Giving Opportunity

Can you give money? Time? More of yourself? How does giving occur in your life? Consider giving more, for example, simply give your best efforts in your daily life. Being open to giving transcends ideas of lack and limitations and opens you up to the true abundance of the heart.

6. Trust

We must trust to not shrink, or to become skittish or cold in our hearts. Instead, with trust, we can soar beyond into places currently unknown. Trust is a gorgeous, special aspect and it can sparkle and be the strongest of ties, like a web of ethereal spiders' silk in the morning sun. We build trust over moments, days, months, years and that is as it should be. The problem can arise when we say or do things that betray that trust. And so, let us choose to grow trust, to believe in it, to nourish and care for trust and then life will be faithful to us. Sub atomically, each particle element of oxygen and hydrogen trusts the other to be there to make up part of a connecting web. And so, we trust there will always be air to breathe. We all live through trust and must not forget this. If you have been hurt, learn to trust again and you will transcend your pain. We were not meant to be hollow, bitter and isolated things.

A Story of Trust

"Don't worry!" he shouted, "I do these 60 times a day and it never gets boring!" Alex was patting my shoulder enthusiastically as the plane door was drawing open and the cold air rushed in to hit my face. I had never sky dived before, but I wasn't scared. I trusted Alex and because of that I was excited. As we wiggled along the front of the plane towards the edge, I saw my leg dangle off the edge towards the ground. But I just listened to Alex as he counted down, "Three, two…" And of course, we went on two, as he later told me that everyone panics on one. We somersaulted out of the plane and into the 60 most adrenaline-fuelled, high-octane seconds of my life. Once we landed safely on the ground, I knew that my trust in Alex had been well placed. At no point, had I felt scared and thanks to him, I had just jumped out of a plane… and survived.

The Trust Opportunity

Do you trust people? To what extent? Do you trust people easily or is it a challenge for you? Reach out and take a chance on someone else. Believe the best in people and give them the opportunity to soar and fly. Without trust, there would be no relationships, no social capital and no real connections. Allow yourself to engage in this most natural of things, reach out and allow trust to develop… You will be amazed at the outcome!

7. Empathy

Who is your brother? How do you feel when you hurt someone? When someone else hurts you? Is there segregation between our thoughts and pain or are they felt in a more interconnected way? I find that the best way to become aware of this is to see humanity's shared connectedness in two ways: the scientific and the moral. Beautifully, all humans are made of the same chemical compounds and particle building blocks.

So, on this level, we are all similar. To take this understanding a bit further, natural wonders such as trees, water and oxygen are also made of the same elements of carbon, helium, and oxygen. So, it is a scientific fact that all beings and matter on our planet and within our universe are made of the same fundamental particles, simply arranged and distributed slightly differently.

Once we understand our shared ancestry and chemical heritage, we can also appreciate life and our similarities in a moral way. As all human beings and living creatures are composed of the same material, we are all related, at this basic, sub atomic level. This offers wonderful possibilities for the ability of our heart, our love for each other and our ability to relate to each other and to all created matter.

Generally, a lot of prejudice, discrimination, ill feeling and hatred come from creating an 'us' and a 'them', a 'familiar' and an 'other' dichotomy. It is one of the most powerfully destructive tools of persuasive rhetoric to convince people that someone else is unfamiliar, different an 'other' that we simply cannot relate to. And yet, as we are made of the very same material, to negate that goes against our very material nature. We should say that there are no idiots that stand alone, unable to relate; there are no monsters, who have been created out of some other sinister materials and who seek to destroy us. There are simply humans and our imaginations. And therein lies great possibility for the heart; for good or for harm.

It is no longer enough to care about just our immediate family, our race, and our species – those who are like us. The Great women and men of our history have shown us that it is in coming together that we embrace the natural abundance and strength within ourselves and within the universe and so become strong: *interacting, accepting, feeling, understanding* and *empathising.*

A Story of Empathy

We had been shopping, bought a lot of stuff and sat down in the Shopping Centre for a coffee. Unexpectedly, a homeless man sat down amongst us and began to talk away. I was surprised but listened to what he had to say. One of the waiters approached from behind and motioned to me, *Did I want him to be moved?* I shook my head and kept listening. He was telling me how difficult it was to find a place to sleep. I was surprised to hear that his favourite place, because it was so quiet, was the graveyard. Although, he said that he had to be careful, as he was often attacked, and he showed me a scar on his face from a knife attack. For twenty minutes or so, I simply listened to this man and experienced his story. I imagined sleeping as he had; I felt feelings of fear, panic, boredom and hopelessness. It was a strongly profound experience. As he left, I thanked him. By simply listening to him, I had shared a strong, profound moment I would not forget, which has developed into a keen urge to combat homelessness.

The Empathy Opportunity

To empathise with others grants us the opportunity to learn from them, to walk in their shoes and to understand both negatively and positively what they are going through. If it is something positive and you can empathise, you can be happy and share in their joy. And if it is awful, then by empathising, you can feel their pain, understand it and help to ease it; if only at first through understanding and being present with someone in their pain.

8. Solidarity
To live in solidarity with each other is to place an arm underneath one another's shoulders and to support each other as we walk together towards a greater freedom.

Solidarity is a powerful way of being with others, even despite physical distance, for example in grief, in loss, in suffering, in disappointment, in times of difficulty. To hold another in our minds and hearts and to seek to help and understand is a great gift to give to them and to the world. There is so much in the world that can cause hurt and confusion, and to stand in solidarity with each other means we value each other and want to experience life together fully, whether good or terrible. It is not only on individual days such as Remembrance Day or at funerals that we can stand in solidarity with each other. It, like patience, is an opportunity present in our everyday lives; we simply need to have the eyes to see it and to embrace it and help others.

A Story of Solidarity

I watched a wonderful documentary about a team of twelve people, who had all lost a large amount of weight, around 100 pounds each. They came together through a new-found love of running, and the film documented their running of a Ragnar Relay; a team race, where each member would do a run, then pass a baton on to the next, with each eventually completing three runs. This moment saw one of the runners attempting a ten mile stretch in the dark at four am. After struggling and walking for several miles, her team caught up with her. Not only did they empathise with her, but with four miles of her part to go, several of them ran an extra mile in her place, to help her and to ease her burden. It was very touching to see the very best of humanity solidarity and support encouragement in the pitch black at the side of a road in the middle of the night.

The Solidarity Opportunity

Suffering is all around us in various ways. It is a part of life that we must embrace and not try to ignore. We must remain open and willing to engage, to empathise, and to stand in solidarity with all people as one family. There is no need for enemies or divisions or petty hatreds anymore. There are too many real issues to face up to that challenge. We must unite. We must be brothers and sisters and allow that shared humanity to drive all that we do. Love the people around you and your influence will grow, because it will no longer just be about you but about us, all of us, together.

9. Support

What supports your life and truly keeps you alive? What grabs you and won't let go? Who can help you when your stomach lurches and all you feel is panic? We are a human group; a single family and our deepest selves know this to be true. All divisions, all separateness disappears in the light of what is truly important. Moments of death, illness and life changing experiences can thrust us together and remind us of what we know deep down to be true: we can be there for each other. Family, friends, colleagues, strangers, all are kin and capable of love. We just tend to forget that sometimes and at our own cost. There is simply no limit to the amount of people that you can support, just as there is no limit to the amount of people that you can have the support of – encouraging, helping and loving you. Every trunk supports thousands of leaves. Every baby is encouraged to smile. Supporting each other is at the very nature of our humanity and our reality as living organisms, what a wonderful way to see our everyday relationships with each other, as part of the symbiotic, inter-related, interdependent natural order and beauty of life.

A Story of Support

He was at his lowest. He left his bed for several hours of relative inactivity each day but not much else. Waves of depression and anxiety came unbidden and engulfed him, disempowering him completely. And yet, she visited him every day. She brought him sandwiches, she made polite talk, she believed in him and held onto hope for him. He could not see it, so she had to see it for him, and for that, in time, he would become very grateful. As she drove away each day, he had a moment each time where he felt a bit better, a bit more capable, and a bit more loved. And for him it kept him going. It was his everything.

The Support Opportunity

Who can you help in your life? Where is the opportunity to add value to someone's life? To reach out beyond ourselves and help others is one of the greatest gifts of life. How will someone be better in their life because of yours? This is a question that I ask myself every day to direct myself and make sure that I am being a worthwhile person. Life is not solely about money or even feeling happy. I believe that supporting, encouraging and developing each other can offer incredible opportunities for all of us to thrive and flourish. Just think of someone who has supported you when you truly needed it, how incredible would it be to be able to provide that for someone else?

10. Vulnerability

When can we feel safe to be vulnerable? With whom and when? If you can answer that, then you have found a rare exquisite treasure of real value, for even mean people have a family and friends. To be vulnerable around someone, is to show them your true self, your moments of weakness, your worst bits. And they still love you! That is a person to keep in your life. So many of us have been taught to never show vulnerability, that being hurt is so bad that you should never allow it to happen again. Toughen up, be a real man, a real woman, don't cry, do it yourself. The problem with all these, usually well-intentioned phrases, is that they offer no framework of how to do this. And worse, they insist that strength is continual and infinite, it is not okay to have moments or periods of weakness, or sadness, or despair, or just not knowing what you are doing. This is completely unhelpful. All my best and most genuine moments of integrity and the best aspects of myself have come after showing and demonstrating weakness. To demonstrate vulnerability requires great courage, no one can stay strong all the time. Do not believe the hype, the social media profiles, the internet highlight reels – people do not often post or discuss their vulnerabilities in any meaningful way. No one has everything figured out, and we do not need to. Accepting our vulnerable moments and areas of our lives can lead to open minded considerations of embracing them, loving ourselves and thriving because of, not instead of, our shared vulnerability as one human family.

A Story of Vulnerability

She had never admitted this to anyone before, and so she shifted from foot to foot as she began talking. Raising her shoulders, then sighing and sagging down into the chair, she began to talk. She listened to her intently, nodding and smiling occasionally, not interrupting. Finally, after tears, tissues and several cups of tea, the whole issue had been laid out bare. She finished talking and for the first time, looked up at her good friend who had been listening and saw only big eyes, a wide grin and deep love. Waves of relief, like a cool breeze, rushed over her face and through her body as she stood up. She couldn't believe that she had not scared her off. Instead, she felt closer to her than ever before.

It is difficult to be vulnerable on purpose. As babies and as children, we all are totally dependent on others at first, and yet as we get older this idea of vulnerability becomes something to be avoiding, to be managed, to not be encouraged. And yet the best, closest and most fulfilling of relationships and moments involve an aspect of vulnerability. Be bold and dare to fail, to take a chance, to be vulnerable and to grow.

The Vulnerability Opportunity

Do you dare to be vulnerable or do you always seek to appear strong and protected? Do you allow yourself to be truly vulnerable and human only with a selected few? Could that be limiting you? Can the willingness to be vulnerable and aware of vulnerability help us to value the beauty of our life and opportunities, as well as allowing us to not be arrogant but humble?

And so here we are: forever grateful and in awe of the deepest of treasures held deep within us – in our hearts. May you always live aware of this most beautiful of treasures, which you carry inside your chest. You are a walking miracle and the wonderful capacity of the heart sings testament to this: the heart can heal, soothe, calm, inspire and ignite. Live through your heart, see and breathe through it and true joy will be a way of life for you. I wish your heart to be healthy, to be joyous and full and to grow stronger each day and bring you deep peace.

Epilogue

The five aspects of our health: the body, the mind, spirit, digital health and our heart are all beautiful opportunities to learn, to love, to develop and grow in a vibrant, spectacular world. I know that with the right attitude, you can surpass your current limitations in whichever way you want. Be persistent, be content, but never be satisfied. Continue to evolve and to be comfortable with change and the world is yours. I wrote this prayer at one of my very lowest moments, wanting to help others in their suffering; which speaks testament to the power and beauty of the loving life force in us.

A Blessing of Health

May your troubles not weigh your body down
May red eyes be wiped clean
And dry, cracked skin be made smooth
May the vibrancy of life ripple through your body
And settle deep inside your heart
May you know the joy of the body's capabilities
To soar, glide, lift and carry
May the whole energy of the stars be yours today
And may you keep this dearest of treasures in your
awareness each and every day

Bonus Materials

Quantum Wonder – How to Appreciate Everyday Life in a Special Way

All things are subject to laws. And yet very small things behave in a completely different way to larger things, and are seemingly outside these laws. This statement is staggering in its enabling of wonder, awe and fascination in the face of the miracle of life. To think of individuals as separate, or objects as whole, suggests separation and isolation. And yet in knowing that everything is made of tiny particles which are surrounded by empty space is fascinating in its ramifications for interaction between us and our world.

No longer can even a plastic bottle be deemed boring or any aspect of life not be infused with a sparkling vibrancy.

For myself, I am enjoying putting on my quantum glasses. When I do, I pause for a moment when surveying a scene or situation. I then consider the atoms that make up the scene, and then the vibrations and frequencies occurring, and then the so-called empty space between them and then what is happening in the electro-magnetic spectrum, and finally what is happening inside the very atoms themselves. I end by zooming back out to survey the scene again afresh and full of a shining specialness and awe that defines words.

The most exciting aspect of this is the stretching that it exerts on the imagination and the sheer baffling nature of what is occurring. There is a terrific connection between all things, in knowing all are made of the same atoms, all follow the laws of the conservation of energy. And that there are the current unknown laws and unknown theories, which will continue to reveal how much that we simply do not know, which we thought we once did. To look at life in a quantum way will absolutely affect your interactions with yourself and others on a daily level. To make time to sit and consider the brilliance of life at a quantum level leads, I feel, to a deeper appreciation of the interconnectedness and absolute magic of being alive and able to acknowledge being so, albeit in a limited way.

In the face of such wonders, aspects such as social interaction, work and play cannot help but be affected. To truly be aware of the building blocks that we all share breaks down any self-imposed notions of race and identity as not false, but transitory and in many ways self-created. And this is okay. There are no right answers to be found in these aspects as such, but I feel that an appreciation of the quantum reality of life can run like a current underneath our daily experiences of life; a surging beautiful river, in which we all swim, and swimming within, we are all equal. To treat another as *an other*, as someone different who is outside of this river is actually a false notion on a quantum level, and so must be recognised as such. This has tremendous possibilities for bringing together unity and interdependence between individuals and groups of people. The vibrations and space which we are made of, all use the same bricks but stack them in completely different ways. There has never been another you and never will be. This is an incredibly joyous prospect as by being alive, one inherits both a special uniqueness and solidarity among the human race and beyond that with the entire existence.

The Quantum Wonder can be used to enrich your appreciation of the beautiful amalgamation of life on an aesthetic level, or as has been discussed, it can take you to a deeper understanding of what it is to be a living thing, never alone and separate in our existence; we are all passengers in the stream. It is my hope that my acknowledgement of life through the Quantum Wonder can enable your appreciation of the temporal nature of things, as well as the special bond which we all share; one of unique tiles in a mosaic that is continually shifting, changing and altering, yet ever magnificent.

The Kind Voice – A Way to Be Kinder to Yourself

There is a voice within us – a small and quiet voice; a voice that is a part of our deepest, fullest selves, not a survival instinct or a thought trail or feeling, but a deep grounding upon which to stand. For a long time, I have found in my work that thoughtful, sensitive and artistic individuals can often show a self-destructive and a nihilistic attitude towards themselves, which cause a lot of pain. There is a feeling, an urge and almost a need to suffer, if not at the hands of others, then of ourselves. This attitude runs contrary to instincts of survival and self-preservation, and can seem to exist only as stopper to happiness, a painful drawing out of the present moment into situations of past and future pain.

However, below and behind this self-destructive howl, is a quiet yet much firmer voice of kindness.

Through thousands of years of survival and evolution on both the level of atoms and cells, animals and now humans, we have adapted and continued to survive and thrive. And we, as modern humans, inherit these thousands of years of biological changes and improvements, energy and cultures. And so, it is no wonder that the mind or the self often feels divided unto itself, wanting some things, needing others, demanding some and hating others. I feel that it is possible for a *socially conscious evolution* that transcends the needs of survival and comes from the individual. This has been occurring over thousands of years, through the improvement of medicine and care and shelter and social attitudes of tolerance and compassion. Though it is indeed true that there is much work to be done, it cannot be denied that in the past five thousand years, great strides have been made in tolerance and empathy towards the attitudes between people of different races, sexuality and religious beliefs. I call for a surging continuation of this, which begins by returning to what I call the voice of kindness.

Deep within is the voice that allows you to rest at home in yourself, to know that you are not rubbish, you are not a failure, and you do not deserve to suffer needlessly.

I think that the need to survive on a physical level as a living being can co-exist with much deeper notions of what that can mean, and happiness and acceptance can be found within this. Due to increasing medical advances, those who may have died due to diseases are living longer, and this has led to a much deeper and richer picture of what it is to be alive and a human in today's world. Beyond discussions of *the right to life* and looking more at *the quality of life*, I feel, can lead us forward; and again, it is driven by this generator of the kind voice within.

To know oneself as much as possible is a goal for many. Yet many of us often struggle with balancing the physical needs of our existence, with understanding who we are, and our rights to life and happiness. And yet I feel that the kind voice within holds the answer. As a living thing, the body has needs which cannot be denied, or we will die. On that very simple level of existence, one becomes forced to look after the body, or die. It is that simple. And so, notions of knowing oneself, happiness and suffering are almost temporarily abandoned to the importance of making sure that the body survives as an entity.

And yet, the great moments of life through art, sport, religion and so many others are not to be found in this singular taking care of a body and its physical needs. The yearnings of the soul, of solidarity and purpose must also be satisfied. So, if we agree that the basic starting point is to care for the body's survival, one must exist on, in spite of one's self, to care for the outer shell, despite the inner conditions of the passenger.

It is like driving a car to a destination, there must be fuel in the tank to arrive at any destination worth going to. So, in caring for the bodies' needs, there is a grudging acceptance that a person is living in this body and it must be cared for, and there is great solace both individually and collectively in this. We are all as humans enduring the same physical condition of humanness, one of solitary bodies, and yet a mass collective experience and this is where the exciting possibilities lie.

So, to begin by looking after the body offers an opportunity to thrive. If the body must be cared for, then the person arrives at a question of the balance of care. How much food shall be eaten? When? What exercise should be performed? When? Simply put, the answers to these questions can be found, tweaked, changed and re-found through a lifetime. But if the inner voice is one of kindness and care towards the individual, then the car is travelling along the right roads, again, regardless of the individual's destinations or lack of them. My inner kind voice now guides me towards balance, wellness and a feeling of personal care and not of relentless driving and relentless ambition.

Moving beyond the bodies' needs, the inner voice of kindness as a lens for interpreting the world can be incredibly beneficial and enabling. For situations and choices, relating them back to the inner voice of kindness makes sure that we have a welcome home in ourselves. Here we can be kind in our thoughts and actions towards ourselves, and simply be. From here we can interpret the world and make decisions that will benefit both ourselves and others:

The truths of the human condition of love, care and compassion are universal.

For example, a kind and loving attitude in our work can allow others to feel enabled and cherished by their very being there. This has astronomical implications for our relationships and daily practices, if we always begin by listening to the voice of kindness towards ourselves and apply this same care and affection towards others. Equally with sexuality, education, religious practise, social justice, if we practice kindness in thought and deed towards ourselves, then that will allow a healthy and fulfilled aspect of ourselves to grow and develop with no need for guilt, shame and hatred of the self.

I do not mean to sound metaphysical or whimsical at all. This notion of the inner voice of kindness is incredibly practical and can be practised every day, with no need for external resources or even other people.

To simply sit and know that kindness towards oneself will benefit both the self and every single living thing is powerfully affirming and a cause for great joy.

It is my hope that I can continue to listen to the inner voice of kindness when the world seems to wear me down, to allow it to permeate through my relationships and into all my practices while I am alive. I believe that the human condition currently offers incredible opportunities for the development of love and acceptance inside the everyday human condition. To know that we are loved and treated kindly by ourselves, allows us to feel valued without the need for another to do it for us. And in doing so, we simply have to treat others as we have been treating ourselves and the chain will continue to grow strong. I know that by treating myself kindly and fully embracing this, I have been able to understand and extend compassion towards others. This I have done from a place of knowing that allows shared space for our different human conditions which all require love, nurturing and affection. With careful care towards ourselves and others, I truly believe that the shared human condition can be led to a place which is richer, deeper, unchartered and truly fantastic.

Daily repeated kindness can work wonders.
What is the purpose of our lives?

What is the purpose of my life? This question has been around my life throughout and has returned again recently. Is there one purpose to my life? Would it help if there was? Do we, as a human race, have a purpose? And what power and influence would a purpose hold anyway? Could it be better to say:

What *does my life mean?*

I do not think that my life has one particular purpose, though I feel that it is full of meaning. These deep notions of *Who am I? Where have I come from? Where am I going?* Are excellent teachers in that they are ageless and formless, capable of fitting every single person at every single point in time: they can never be answered fully, and yet, they feel the need to be asked time and time again. To be alive is a blessing. For me it is, I am not writing on the behalf of others, I am speaking of my experience. To even exist is an incredible gift; the odds of existing at this point and place in time are approximately 1 in 13 trillion. Does that give me purpose? Does it give me meaning? Well yes, it does. I feel that the where have I come from question is essential in helping us to understand that there was a time before us, the universe existed and functioned without needing us. And the where am I going question is answered in death.

So, we have come from nothing and will return to nothing, how does that help us to interpret the final question of *Who am I? What is my purpose or meaning in life?* To answer this, I will turn to suffering.

As Buddha said, to live involves suffering, it is a fact and an essential of life in our universe. Victor Frankl interpreted suffering both powerfully and beautifully, when he said that although a terrible act of situation may not have a purpose or reason; one is always free to find a meaning not of it, but through it. I love this and the notion of meaning through suffering has brought me on leaps in the appreciation of who I am and the wondrous existence of daily life. My sufferings in life have taught me, moulded me and have been my best teachers. These have ranged from physical illness, through relationship problems to death. And they have caused me immense physical, emotional and spiritual pain. And yet, these sharp experiences have carved, although painfully, a space in my soul that can now be filled with possibility. They destroyed previous feeble innocent notions and replaced them with a void. And it is into this void that life can begin to flow, as it did in its beginning. We are always free to create a meaning, to forge a purpose, as ultimately, all questions of meaning and purpose will be meaningless in the face of death; and yet, they can power an individual through their entire lifetime, if strong enough.

And so, to return to the original question, *what is the purpose of my life?* The answer is to be found outside the question answer dichotomy. Just as all opposites are ultimately part of the one whole, any question answered will ultimately be proven insufficient in the light of further evidence and discoveries. Purposes and meaning will shift with time as they should do, and yet, our deeds will remain.

Between the two empty voids our *life existence* is purpose and meaning enough to carry us through the dark and beyond the stars to a new home.

Loving Kindness Poem

My body is a great hearth, brimming with warmth
My soul is a vibrant rose, emanating beauty and sweetness
Inside the dark shell of my body is a burning candle, a resounding yes
Each breath sings an affirmation
Of acceptance and joy in solitude
My being is abundant
I can count every one of my smiles
My hope carries me
Through the wind and beyond the stars
Into a future as prosperous as a fruit tree
My soul dances in the night, speaks in the halls of slumber
and rises after every defeat
No one can take my heart

Final Suggestions

My final suggestion to you in the way of Kataholistic Health is to begin a gratitude journal. Every day, write down three things that you are grateful for, no matter what the day has brought. There are many excellent videos and articles written on this subject, which you can find online. For me, beginning a gratitude journal lead to the book you are now reading.

I begin by writing the three grateful things, and then I add photographs from the day with captions. Then I begin to look forward to writing and it leads me to consider my day more deeply, to ask questions and to reflect more. This allows me to write down much more inspiring and thoughtful material. I do not write mundane details of what I do each day. Instead, I focus on gratitude and from there I explore ideas, concepts, problems both big and small, my feelings and my sense of purpose. It then becomes a great joy to write.

You can begin with a simple notepad or paper. Or you can write it on your phone, which will give you access to your photos and any information that you may want to research. Whatever feels natural and comfortable for you is the best way. And, I find that the best way to approach it is with no expectations of words count, style or even subject. Just show up and see what happens. I do recommend that you write your journal at a set time of the day. I began my journal in the evening, just before I went to sleep. This has now led me to write in the morning as well. I found that when I look back, it can be fun to explore contrasts in style and tone. Take the time to look back at previous weeks and to think forward to the future too. I have found that my best ideas, favourite moments, worst failures and some of my deepest reflections are all in your journal. And yours can be too!

A journal will never criticise you. It will never belittle you or tell you your dreams and aspirations are *not realistic*. Instead, it will listen; offer a generous space for you to be yourself in private and to nourish yourself daily. It is very satisfying to look back through your year and see it in three different ways: through feelings of gratitude, through the eyes of pictures and through the words of the soul. Enjoy the process of writing as you will get to know yourself better through it and may even surprise yourself with some of the things looking back at you from the page. It is a wonderful practice to begin. So, start today.

My name is Michael and I no longer believe in limits. I have so far been a teacher, personal trainer, coach, musician, artist, poet, actor, consultant, speaker and author. I love people and I believe that the best is still to come for all of us, working together interdependently from a place of mutual respect, understanding and love.